To the Children of The Fay School —

Nancy White Carlstrom
Best Wishes
& Happy Dreams!

Nancy White Carlstrom

Nov. 17, 1993

NORTHERN LULLABY

Illustrated by *Leo and Diane Dillon*

Philomel Books · New York

Library of Congress Cataloging-in-Publication Data
Carlstrom, Nancy White.   Northern lullaby/by Nancy Carlstrom. p.   cm.
Summary: A child says goodnight to the natural world and all those that occupy it.
ISBN 0-399-21806-8 1. Lullabies, American. 2. Children's poetry, American.
[1. Bedtime—Poetry. 2. Nature—Poetry. 3. Lullabies. 4. American poetry.] I. Title.
PS3553.A7355N67   1991 811'.54—dc20   90-19719   CIP   AC

First Impression

For my family
remembering Rosie Creek
and our first Alaskan winter
N.W.C.

To the family of Earth
L. & D.D.

Goodnight Papa Star
Goodnight Mama Moon,
Bending your silver arms
    down through the darkness.

Goodnight Grandpa Mountain
In shimmering robe,
Straighten your nightcap
of new-fallen snow.

Goodnight Grandma River
Frozen below
With lullaby ripples
    of pale gleaming light.

Goodnight Great Moose Uncle
And Wolf Uncle Gray,
Snowshoe Hare play
    as you move beyond shadows.

Goodnight Auntie Willow
Goodnight Auntie Birch,
Standing in long flannel
gowns in the silence.

Goodnight Cousins Beaver
Deer Mouse and Red Fox,
Nodding in snug homes
protected from ice.

Goodnight Sister Owl
Quiet your cry,
Fold the night sky close
    under dark feathers.

Goodnight Brother Bear
Already asleep,
Peaceful and warmed
    by your deep song of winter.

Shine down Mama Moon
Shine down Papa Star,
Wrap me in your soft quilt
 of stillness tonight.

And when I turn over
Between sleep and dreams,
Northern Lights dance
   your goodnight over me.

Goodnight.

Goodnight.